Copyright © 2024 Angela A. Sparks
ISBN 978-0-9756469-0-8
All rights reserved.

Disclaimer; The information presented in this book is the author's opinion and does not represent any professional advice. The content of this book is for recreational purposes only and is at the readers discretion. Neither the publisher nor the author is engaged in rendering professional advice or services to the reader. The ideas and suggestions, provided in this book are not intended as a substitute for seeking professional guidance.

Preface

The 'Love Journal' was specially designed for those who want to capture the exhilarating and transformative moments within their romantic relationship and for those in pursuit of self-discovery.
The concept for the 'Love Journal' transpired after years of observation and numerous discussions shared.
Upon reflection on the various stages of life, love, and relationships, the enthusiastically happy moments and the tearful ones, searching high and low for solutions to our unique circumstances.
I came to the conclusion that a journal such as this, would greatly benefit many, illuminating what matters most.
The 'Love Journal' provides the perfect tools that are required to allow you to fully express yourself, without reservation. Creating a private space to write down your innermost thoughts as they arise, with guides and prompts to help you clarify your deepest feelings. Journalling will enable you to gain insight and enhance your understanding of your partner and yourself. Writing about your romantic relationship can help define your strengths and weaknesses as a couple. In addition, the 'Love Journal' has dedicated sections to preserve cherished memories and precious moments. With decorative love symbology throughout and deeply felt poetry, the 'Love Journal' creates the ideal opportunity to embrace the wonder and ultimate journey of life and love.

Photos

Date: ....

Name: ....

Age: ....

Date: ....

Name: ....

Age: ....

....

....

....

How We Met

Date: _____

Date:

First Date

Date:

Whispers Of Love,
Carry Warmth And
Kindness On The Soft
Wings Of A Butterfly.
Thoughtful And Sweet,
Like A Gentle
Summer Breeze
Brushing Against
My Cheeks.
Tenderly Caressing,
Igniting My Heart,
Bringing Forth A
Rush Of Love And Desire.
And Yet, A Sense
Of Peaceful Certainty
Nurtures My Soul,
An Echo Of Joy In My
Heart, As The Moonlit Sky.

Date:

Legend:
Is your love on fire, or getting you down?

Love On Fire Exhilaration		Exciting, Joyful Passionate
Deep Love Quality Time		Deep Passion No.1 Priority
Joy, Laughter In Love		Content, Trust Best Friends
Friend Zone Bored		Dull Stuck
Confused Mistrust		Anxious Disappointed
Sadness Lonely, Empty		Frustrated Annoyed
In Despair Betrayal, Fearful		Angry, Hatred Broken Hearted

Love Gauge

Fill in one sector of the pattern below with a colour from the adjacent page, that matches your emotions on any given day.
If the pattern over time, is filled with pink and red tones, you are in a happy, loving relationship. If the pattern is filled with a mixture of colours, there may be some areas in your relationship that need your attention.

On the other hand if your colours are predominantly green, blue, grey and black, it may be time to sit down and have a serious conversation with your partner, and discuss the areas that need to be adjusted. If you are both unable to resolve the issues, you may want to consider if this relationship is right for you.

Date: ....

Love Language

What Makes You Feel Loved?

 Receiving Cuddles
Kissing Passionately
Holding Hands
Physical Love & Intimacy
Feeling Nurtured
Feeling Valued
Laughing Together
 Feeling Safe & Protected
Being Made A Priority
Words of Appreciation
Words of Encouragement
Feeling Supported
Respectful Conversation
Feeling Listened To
Quality Time Together
 Cooking Meals Together
Being Helpful
Contributing At Home
Remembering Likes &
Dislikes, Important Dates
Receiving Flowers, Gifts
Being Wined & Dined
Being Provided For
Intellectual Conversation
Going On Holidays Together
Sharing Common Interests
Partner Making An Effort
Feeling Proud To Be By Your Side

Date:

 # Keepsakes

Date: .... Date: ....

Date: .... Date: ....

Date:

Love At First Sight, Obsession And Our Brain

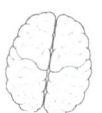

Have you ever met someone and had an instant romantic attraction to them? After your first encounter, they are constantly on your mind? You have an undeniable desire to get to know them on a personal level, and there is a very strong chemistry between you. These intense emotions can cause a rush of love hormones, especially in the early stages of a new relationship? A bizarre phenomenon associated with these emotions, can reduce a person's cognitive function when in the presence of their love interest, rendering them incoherent, speechless, and literally shaking at the knees. If you have ever experienced any of these symptoms, you are not alone. A feeling of helplessness and despair, followed by immense embarrassment may arise, as you struggle to make sense of what is happening to you. Hopefully, if the person causing you these involuntary reactions cares for you ever so slightly, they will be thoughtful, kind and understanding. They may feel touched at your reaction to them, and deem you adorable. Or they may find you awkward, and the situation very uncomfortable, struggling to make a connection with you, it could be; Au Revoir!

Significant Dates

Date:

Date:

Date:

Date:

Date:

Date:

Date:

As Your
Fingertips Gently
Trace My Face,
We Share A
Passionate Kiss And
A Loving Embrace.
Our Love Begins
To Blossom.

A Sweet
Loving Whisper,
With Adoring
Eyes, Gazing
Deeply Into Mine.
Filling My Heart
With Excitement,
And Joy, Igniting A
Passion Of
Unquenchable
Desires.

Significant Dates

Date:

Date:

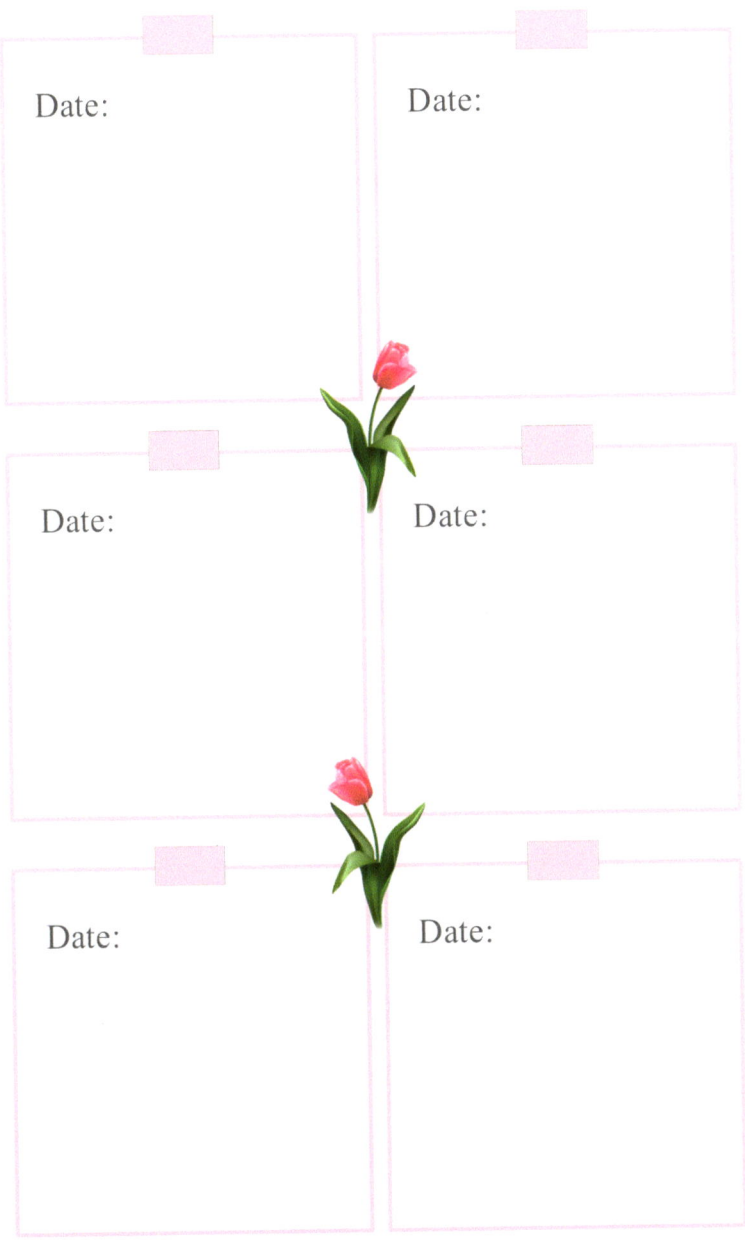

Date:

Date:

Date:

Date:

Date: ....

The Language Of Love,
Is Expressed In The Silent,
Tender Moments,
Secretly Hidden Away
In Ones Heart.

Mood Monitor

Mark a dot alongside an Emoji that conveys your mood today. Sit with this feeling, listen to your heart, give yourself gentle acceptance.

Date:

 # Keepsakes

Date: _____   Date: _____

Date: _____   Date: _____

Gratitude

Being grateful for all that is positive in our lives is a key ingredient to feeling happy and content. List the areas specifically relating to your relationship that you are grateful for.

♥ ☐
♥ ☐
♥ ☐
♥ ☐
♥ ☐
♥ ☐
♥ ☐

Mutual Point
Of View

Date: ....

Date: ....

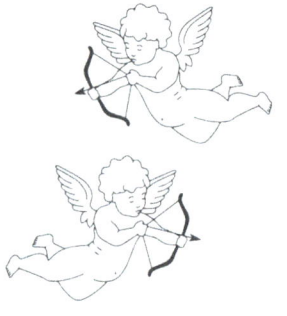

My Love For You
Is Deeper Than
The Ocean,
My Heart Races
Whenever You
Are Near.
Your Smile
Brightens My Day
And Your Laughter
Fills My Heart
With Such Joy.
I Shall Never
Tire Of You.

Opposing View Point

Date:

Date:

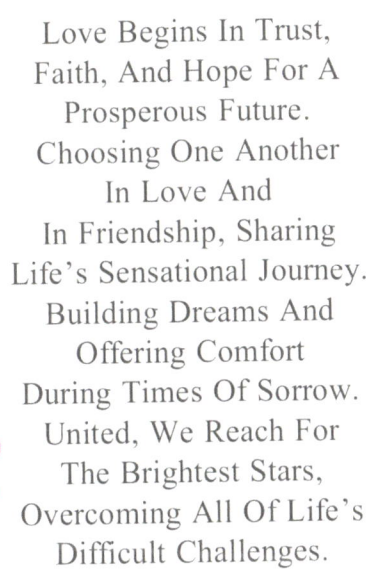

Love Begins In Trust,
Faith, And Hope For A
Prosperous Future.
Choosing One Another
In Love And
In Friendship, Sharing
Life's Sensational Journey.
Building Dreams And
Offering Comfort
During Times Of Sorrow.
United, We Reach For
The Brightest Stars,
Overcoming All Of Life's
Difficult Challenges.

Weekend Activities

What pastimes do you enjoy as individuals, and as a couple?

Relaxing, Reading A Book
Cafe Breakfast, Brunch, Lunch, Dinner
Movie Night, Popcorn & Icecream
Visiting Friends & Family
Dinner Party, Birthday Party, Wedding
Shop Until You Drop, Exploring The City
Fish & Chips On The Beach
A Long Drive To Nowhere
Dog walking, Bushwalking, Hiking
Bicycle Rides, Skating, Skateboarding
Visits To Historical Country Towns
Wineries & Wine Tasting, Open Fires
Art Galleries, Museums, Libraries
Theatre, Ballet, Recital
Drinks At The Local Pub or Bar
Live Bands, Concerts, Stand Up Comedy
Dancing All Night At A Club
Football Game, Tennis, Cricket, Golf
Gym Workouts, Fitness, Training
Running, Cross Country Running
Camping, Caravanning, BBQ Cook Up
Swimming, Pool, Lake, River Or Beach
Fishing Trips, Snorkeling, Scuba Diving
Surfing, Jet Skiing, Other Water Sports
Yachting, Sailing, Canoeing, Or Rowing
Skiing, Snowboarding, Visit the Snow
Gaming, Computer, Phone, Social Media
Working, Business, Marketing, Networking

Date:

Imperfect Beauty

A Brilliant
Cut Diamond Has
Many Facets.
Colours Of The
Rainbow Adorn
Its Surface.
Gloriously
Forming Mosaics,
Refracting Light,
Shining Ever Bright.
Eternally Sparkling,
Though Deep Within,
Lies Its Raw
Imperfect Beauty.

Date:

Character / Values

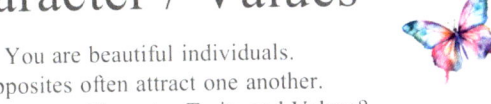

You are beautiful individuals.
Opposites often attract one another.
What are your Character Traits and Values?

- Adventurous vs Wary
- Artistic vs Uninspired
- Charitable vs Self Interest
- Conviction vs Easily Swayed
- Commitment vs Noncommittal
- Cooperation vs Aggressiveness
- Courteous vs Discourteous
- Courageous vs Fearful
- Determination vs Quitter
- Diplomacy vs Violence
- Dynamic vs Stagnant
- Equality vs Inequality
- Excellence vs Mediocre
- Fairness vs Injustice
- Family vs Independence
- Fixed vs Flexible
- Forgiving vs Blaming
- Fun vs Dull
- Generosity vs Selfish
- Giver vs Taker
- Gratitude vs Ungrateful
- Hard Working vs Lazy
- Healthy vs Unhealthy
- Honesty vs Dishonest
- Humble vs Boastful
- Innovative vs Inaction
- Integrity vs Devious
- Kindness vs Cruelty
- Order vs Misconduct
- Learning vs Ignorance
- Love vs Hatred
- Loyalty vs Infidelity
- Marriage Vs Single
- Modest vs Seeking Power
- Organised vs Untidy
- Patience vs Frustration
- Patriotism vs Treachery
- Peace vs Chaos
- Protest vs Silence
- Quiet solitude vs Noisy
- Reliable vs Unreliable
- Religious vs Atheist
- Humour vs Seriousness
- Spiritual vs Secular
- Timely vs Constantly Late
- Travelling vs Settled
- Truth vs Deceit
- Trustworthy vs Shameless
- Understanding vs Uncaring
- Witty vs Sarcasm

Date: ....

In Your Eyes, I See The Stars,
Forever Glistening.
You Are My Guiding Light.
Your Unequivocal Love Soothes
My Deepest Pain.
Your Strength Shields Me From
The Storm, Thunder And Rain.
Your Presence Gives Me Peace
Of Mind. You Are My Safe
Haven, My Heart's Eternal
Valentine.

Date:

Legend:
Is your love on fire, or getting you down?

Love On Fire Exhilaration	♥	Exciting, Joyful Passionate
Deep Love Quality Time	♥	Deep Passion No.1 Priority
Joy, Laughter In Love	♥	Content, Trust Best Friends
Friend Zone Bored	♥	Dull Stuck
Confused Mistrust	♥	Anxious Disappointed
Sadness Lonely, Empty	♥	Frustrated Annoyed
In Despair Betrayal, Fearful	💔	Angry, Hatred Broken Hearted

Love Gauge

Fill in one sector of the pattern below with a colour from the adjacent page, that matches your emotions on any given day.
If the pattern over time, is filled with pink and red tones, you are in a happy, loving relationship. If the pattern is filled with a mixture of colours, there may be some areas in your relationship that need your attention.

On the other hand if your colours are predominantly green, blue, grey and black, it may be time to sit down and have a serious conversation with your partner, and discuss the areas that need to be adjusted. If you are both unable to resolve the issues, you may want to consider if this relationship is right for you.

Personal Dreams And Goals

We are all unique, including our Dreams and Goals. Mark your dreams and goals and note any additions on the adjacent page.

- 7 Wonders of the World
- Become a Pet Owner
- Build a Share Portfolio
- Buy a Block of Land
- Buy a Penthouse
- Buy My Dream Car
- Buy My Dream Home
- Compete In The Olympics
- Create a Vegetable Garden
- Design and Sew My Clothes
- Drive a Sports Car
- Exercise Regularly
- Fly a Plane or Helicopter
- Get Married, Start a Family
- Get My Black Belt
- Go Bungy Jumping
- Go Rock Climbing
- Go Parachuting
- Go Scuba Diving
- Host a Dinner Party
- Join A Gym
- Join a Martial Art Class
- Join a Sporting Team
- Join a Yoga Class
- Learn to Cook
- Learn a Musical Instrument
- Learn Another Language
- Learn to Knit or Sew
- Learn to Sing
- Learn to Ski or Snowboard
- Live in the Countryside
- Live Overseas
- Lose Weight
- Meet a Celebrity
- Move Interstate
- Plant a Tree
- Public Speaking
- Ride a Bicycle
- Ride a Motorbike
- Run a Marathon
- Sail The Seas
- Start My Own Business
- Swim 20 Laps
- Take a Dancing Lesson
- Take an Art Class
- Take up Photography
- Tone Up My Body
- Travel Interstate
- Travel The World
- Visit Niagara Fall
- Visit The Grand Canon
- Volunteer for Charity
- Work Overseas
- Write & Publish A Book

Date: ....

 # Keepsakes

Date: _____ Date: _____

Date: _____ Date: _____

Date: ....

Mood Monitor

Mark a dot alongside an Emoji that conveys your mood today. Sit with this feeling, listen to your heart, give yourself gentle acceptance.

Date:

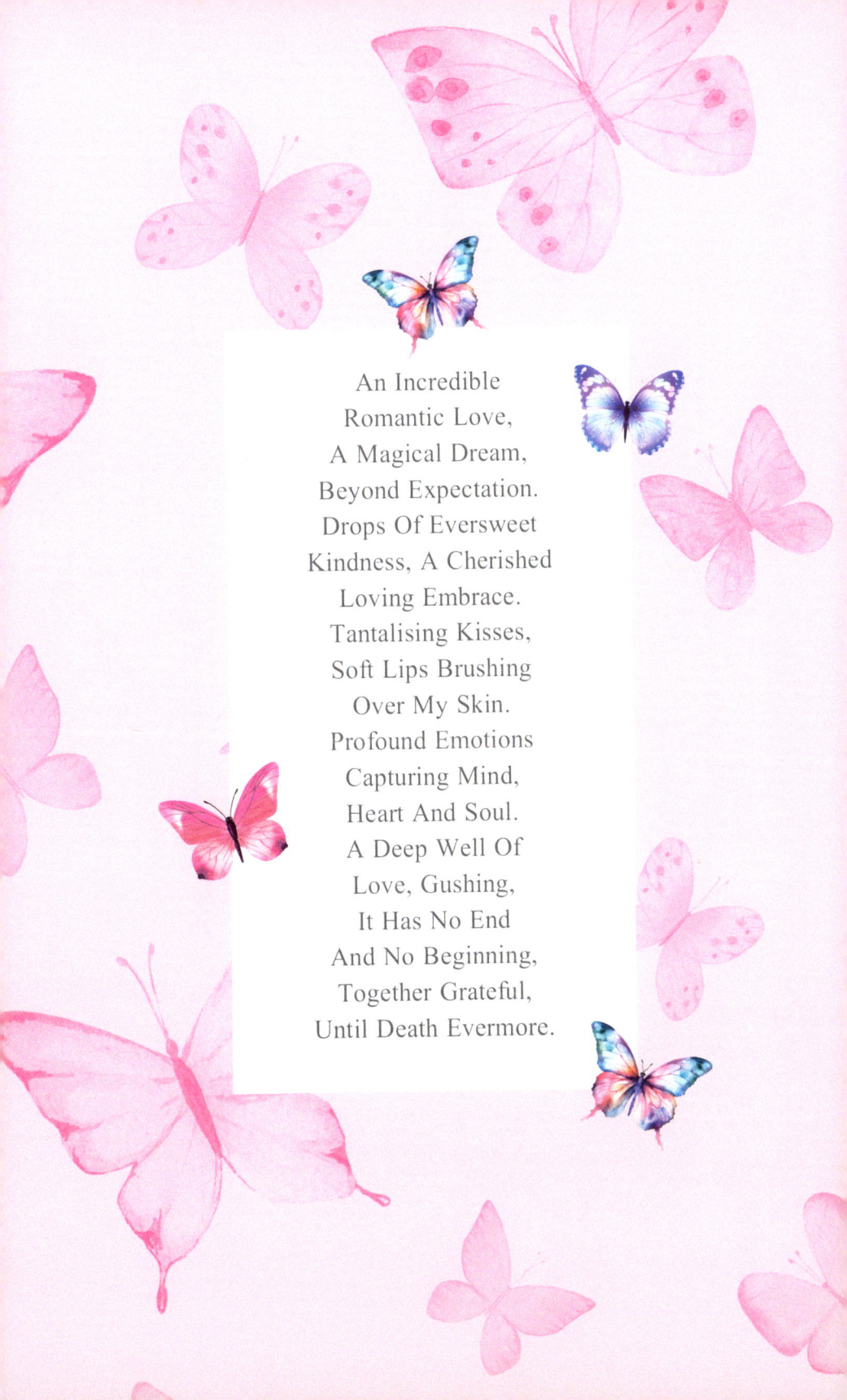

An Incredible
Romantic Love,
A Magical Dream,
Beyond Expectation.
Drops Of Eversweet
Kindness, A Cherished
Loving Embrace.
Tantalising Kisses,
Soft Lips Brushing
Over My Skin.
Profound Emotions
Capturing Mind,
Heart And Soul.
A Deep Well Of
Love, Gushing,
It Has No End
And No Beginning,
Together Grateful,
Until Death Evermore.

Date:

You Have The Key To My Heart,
It Belongs To You.
Be Careful Not To Break It.

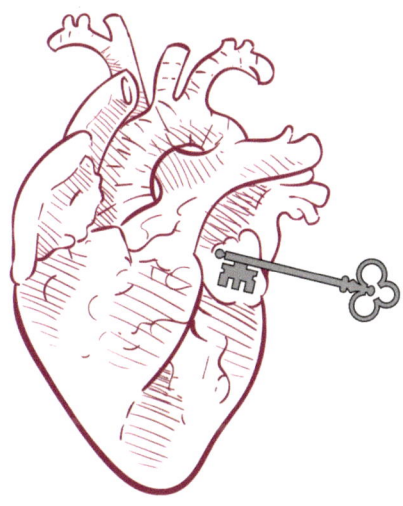

For In Your Presence, I Wish To Be.
Let Our Profound Love Take Flight,
Let Our Lives Not Be In Vain.

Photos

Date:

Name:

Age:

Date:

Name:

Age:

Past Hurts

Feeling hurt or mistreated can impact your wellbeing. We can unintentionally bring these painful emotions to the surface, which can impact our relationships. Write down the most painful experiences in your life, acknowledge and release these emotions. Reliving painful experiences will burden you and those around you. If possible try and live in the present, and be mindful of your thoughts.

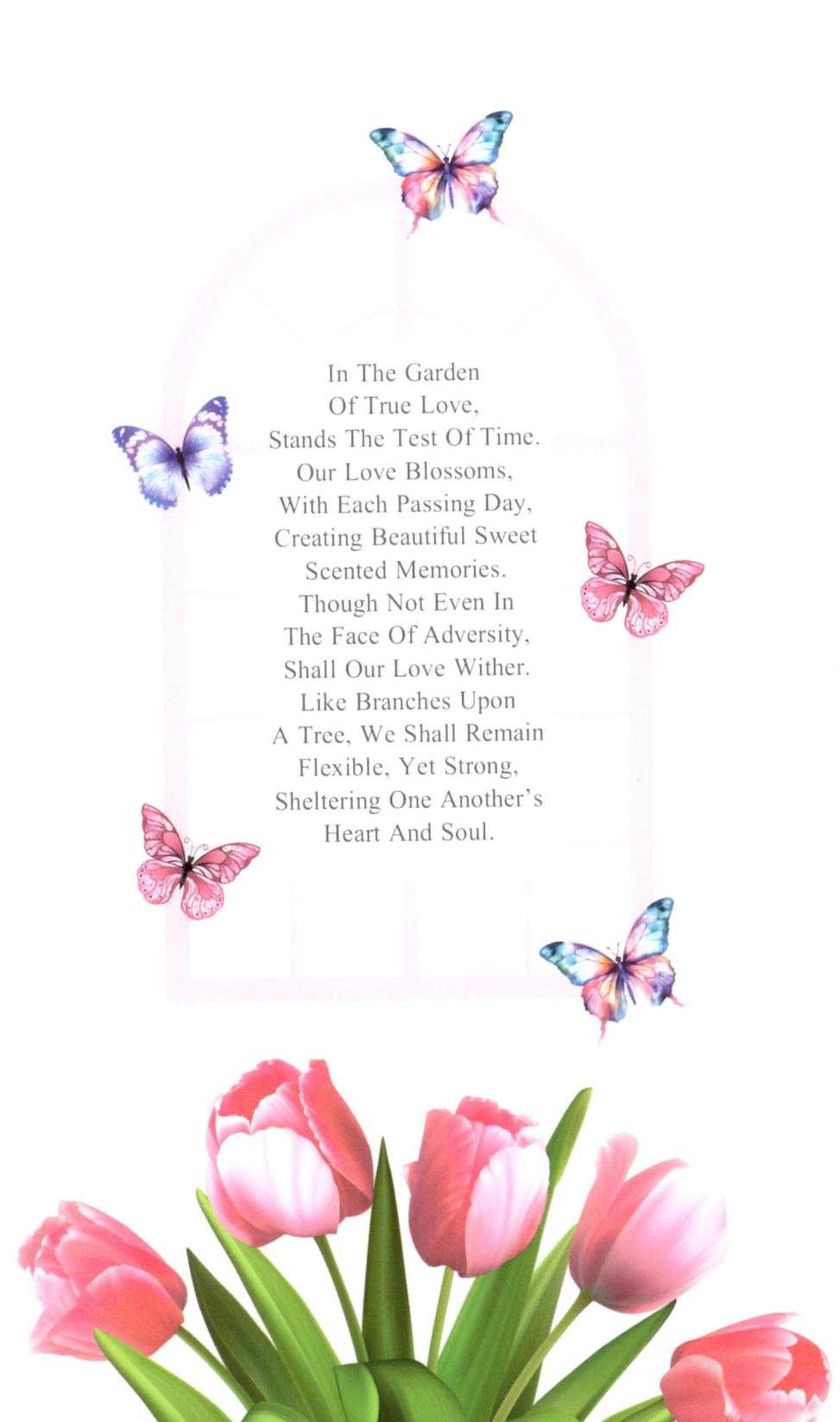

In The Garden
Of True Love,
Stands The Test Of Time.
Our Love Blossoms,
With Each Passing Day,
Creating Beautiful Sweet
Scented Memories.
Though Not Even In
The Face Of Adversity,
Shall Our Love Wither.
Like Branches Upon
A Tree, We Shall Remain
Flexible, Yet Strong,
Sheltering One Another's
Heart And Soul.

Date:

I See You. All Of You.
I Love You, More Than You Will
Ever Know, Despite Your Faults.
I Feel Your Presence In The
Distance As You Approach.
My Heart Unsure Of What Is To Be.
The Memories Of You Linger,
They Shall Be Engraved
Upon My Heart,
Until It Beats
No More.

 # Keepsakes

Date: _____   Date: _____

Date: _____   Date: _____

Date:

Love Is Patient,
And Kind,
Tender And Faithful.
Love Heals All
Suffering,
And Wipes Away
Our Countless Tears.
Love Fills Our Hearts
With Pure Bliss And
A Gentle Calm,
Embedded
In Our Soul.
Love Perseveres,
Even When Life
Throws Its Rocks
And Arrows.

Date:

Our Heartbeat,
A Perfect Ballad.

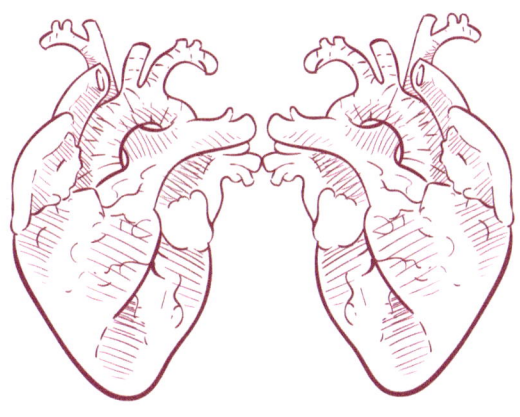

Creating A Unique Love Song,
That Only We Can Hear.

Date:

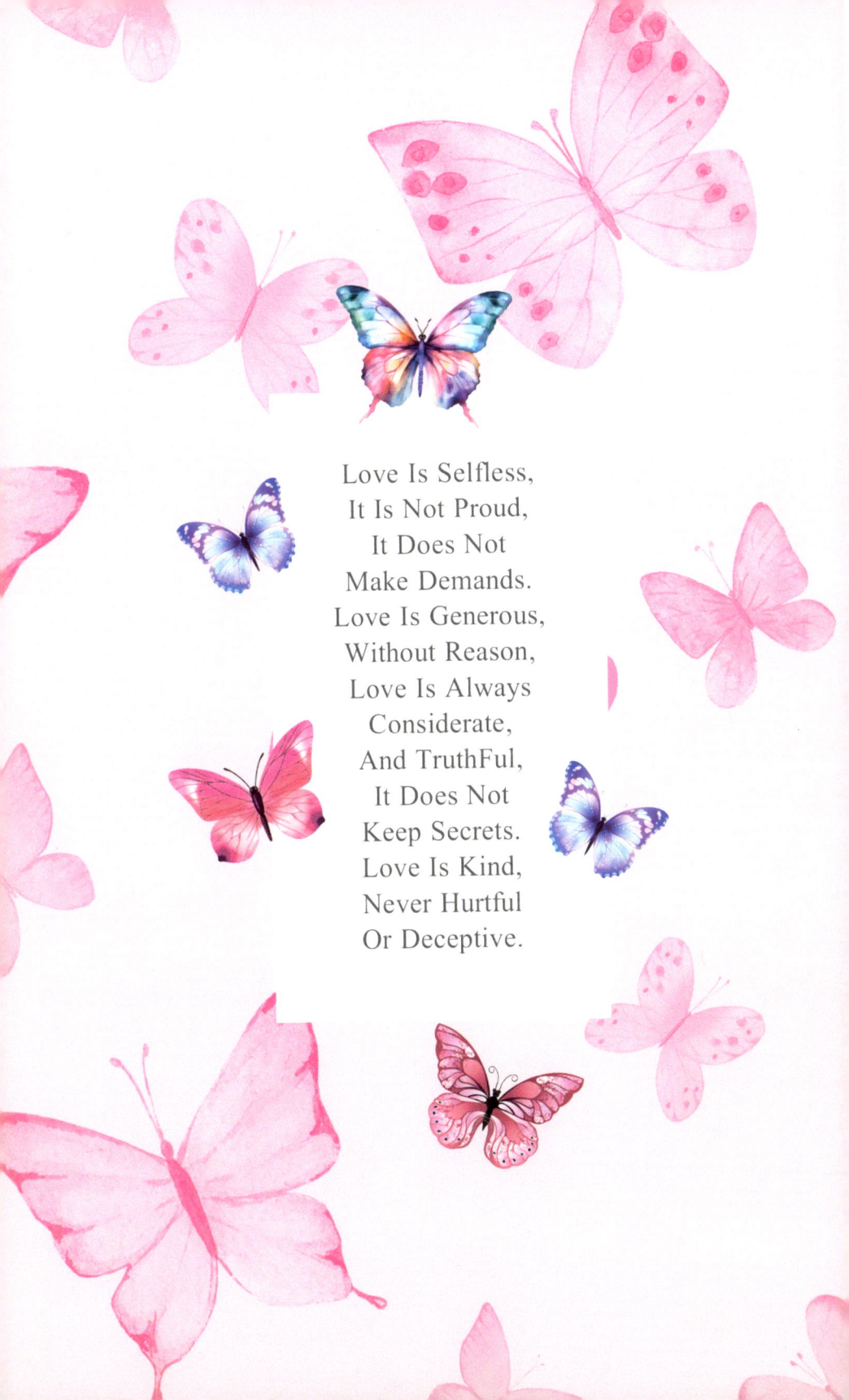

Love Is Selfless,
It Is Not Proud,
It Does Not
Make Demands.
Love Is Generous,
Without Reason,
Love Is Always
Considerate,
And TruthFul,
It Does Not
Keep Secrets.
Love Is Kind,
Never Hurtful
Or Deceptive.

Date:

 # Keepsakes

Date: _____   Date: _____

Date: _____   Date: _____

Date:

Mood Monitor

Mark a dot alongside an Emoji that conveys your mood today. Sit with this feeling, listen to your heart, give yourself gentle acceptance.

Date: ....

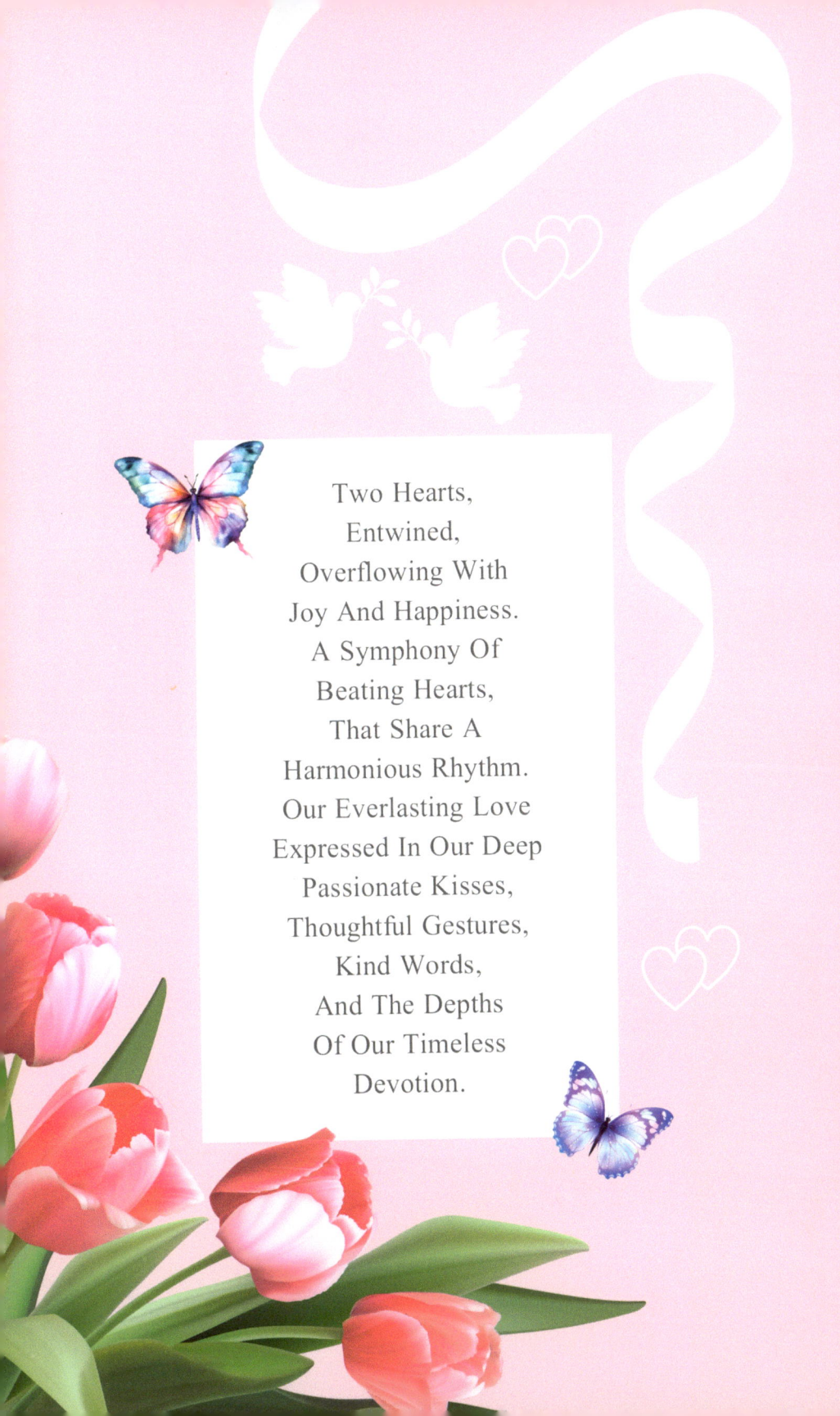

Two Hearts,
Entwined,
Overflowing With
Joy And Happiness.
A Symphony Of
Beating Hearts,
That Share A
Harmonious Rhythm.
Our Everlasting Love
Expressed In Our Deep
Passionate Kisses,
Thoughtful Gestures,
Kind Words,
And The Depths
Of Our Timeless
Devotion.

Date:

Engaged

Love, A Deep Affection,
Followed By Commitment To
One Another, And An
Unwavering Adoration.

Engaged

Date: _____

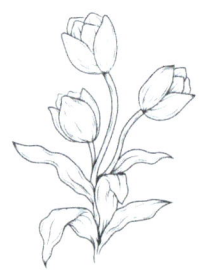

Photos

Date: ....

Name: ....

Age: ....

Date: ....

Name: ....

Age: ....

Legend:
Is your love on fire, or getting you down?

Love On Fire Exhilaration		Exciting, Joyful Passionate
Deep Love Quality Time		Deep Passion No.1 Priority
Joy, Laughter In Love		Content, Trust Best Friends
Friend Zone Bored		Dull Stuck
Confused Mistrust		Anxious Disappointed
Sadness Lonely, Empty		Frustrated Annoyed
In Despair Betrayal, Fearful		Angry, Hatred Broken Hearted

Love Gauge

Fill in one sector of the pattern below with a colour from the adjacent page, that matches your emotions on any given day.
If the pattern over time, is filled with pink and red tones, you are in a happy, loving relationship. If the pattern is filled with a mixture of colours, there may be some areas in your relationship that need your attention.

On the other hand if your colours are predominantly green, blue, grey and black, it may be time to sit down and have a serious conversation with your partner, and discuss the areas that need to be adjusted. If you are both unable to resolve the issues, you may want to consider if this relationship is right for you.

Date:

Married

Forever & Ever

Married

Date: ....

Photos

Date: ....

Name: ....

Age: ....

Date: ....

Name: ....

Age: ....

....

....

....

Date:

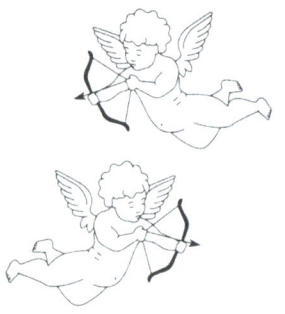

Eternal Love
Captures The Depths
Of My Being.
My Thoughts Of You
Linger Night And Day.
Your Eyes Pierce
My Soul,
Your Smile Lights
Up My World.
In Your Embrace,
I Find Refuge.
You Are My
True Love,
My Heart Is
Now Whole.

 # Keepsakes

Date: .... Date: ....

Date: .... Date: ....

Date: ....

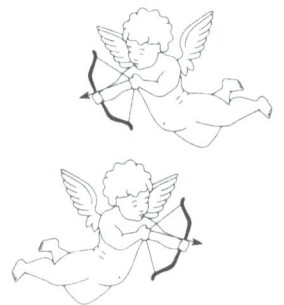

www.ingramcontent.com/pod-product-compliance
Lightning Source LLC
Chambersburg PA
CBHW042049290426
44110CB00001B/5